ICONS

DDR
DESIGN

EAST GERMAN DESIGN
DESIGN DE LA RDA

DDR DESIGN

EAST GERMAN DESIGN
DESIGN DE LA RDA
1949–1989

Fotos/Photos: Ernst Hedler
Einleitung/Introduction: Ralf Ulrich

TASCHEN

KÖLN LONDON LOS ANGELES MADRID PARIS TOKYO

Logo der Jungen Pioniere/Logo of the Young
Pioneers: "Be Prepared"/Le logo des Jeunes
Pionniers : « Soyez Prêts »

Umschlagvorderseite/Front cover/ Couverture:
Schaufensterdekoration/Window display/
Décoration de vitrine

Umschlagrückseite & Seite 2/Back cover & page 2/
Dos de couverture & page 2:
Emblem der SED/Emblem of the SED/
Emblème du SED

© 2004 TASCHEN GmbH
Hohenzollernring 53, D-50672 Köln
www.taschen.com

Photos by Ernst Hedler
Photos by Hans-Martin Sewcz on pages: 10/11,
12, 16, 20/21, 30/31, 32/33, 114/115; 128/129
English translation: Isabel Varea for
Grapevine Publishing, London
French translation: Michèle Schreyer, Cologne
Editorial coordination: Annick Volk, Cologne
Design: Catinka Keul, Cologne
Production: Ute Wachendorf, Cologne

Printed in Italy
ISBN 3-8228-3216-2

INHALT
CONTENTS
SOMMAIRE

6 EINLEITUNG

12 INTRODUCTION

16 INTRODUCTION

24 NAHRUNGSMITTEL, GENUSSMITTEL
FOOD, LUXURY ITEMS
PRODUITS ALIMENTAIRES, DENREES DE LUXE

58 HAUSHALTSWAREN
HOUSEHOLD GOODS
ARTICLES MENAGERS

94 ELEKTRISCHE, TECHNISCHE, OPTISCHE GERÄTE
ELECTRICAL, TECHNICAL, OPTICAL INSTRUMENTS
APPAREILS ELECTRIQUES, TECHNIQUES, OPTIQUES

112 REINIGUNGSMITTEL, HYGIENEBEDARF
CLEANSING PRODUCTS, COSMETICS
PRODUITS DE NETTOYAGE, PRODUITS COSMETIQUES

148 PAPIERE, STOFFE, BÜROBEDARF
PAPER GOODS, MATERIAL, STATIONERY
PAPIERS, TISSUS, PAPETERIE

172 SPIELWAREN
TOYS
JOUETS

188 GESCHICHTLICHER ÜBERBLICK
HISTORY OF EAST GERMAN DESIGN
HISTOIRE DU DESIGN EN RDA

EINLEITUNG

Im Sommer 1989 eröffnete die Galerie Habernoll in Dreieich bei Frankfurt am Main die Ausstellung „SED – Schönes Einheitsdesign". Die beiden Kuratoren Matthias Dietz und Christian Habernoll präsentierten eine umfangreiche Sammlung von Alltagsprodukten aus der DDR. Die westdeutsche Öffentlichkeit erhielt dabei nicht nur einen Einblick in die Konsumwelt eines fremden Landes, sondern indirekt wurden die Besucher auch mit der eigenen Nachkriegszeit konfrontiert: Zahlreiche der ausgestellten DDR-Produkte erinnerten aus westdeutscher Perspektive an eine ferne, längst vergangene Zeit, die noch nicht von aufwändigen Marketingstrategien und raffiniertem Verpackungsdesign geprägt war. Mit dem Fall der Mauer und der Währungsunion im Juni 1990 gerieten Ost-Produkte wie der Trabbi, Club-Cola, Juwel-Zigaretten und Spee-Waschmittel in unmittelbare Konkurrenz zum VW-Golf, Coca-Cola, Camel und Ariel. Zumindest in ihrer damaligen Qualität und Form konnten die Produkte der DDR-Wirtschaft kaum mehr bestehen. Innerhalb einer kurzen Zeitspanne mutierten sie zu Fossilien eines untergegangenen Wirtschafts- und Gesellschaftssystems.

Die hier abgebildeten Produkte sind ein Schaufenster der Konsumkultur der DDR. Der verstaubte Charme ihrer Formen und ihrer Verpackungen fasziniert den heutigen Betrachter; zugleich sind sie Dokumente einer Stagnation, die nicht unwesentlich zum Scheitern der DDR beigetragen hat. Die sozialistische Formgebung oder Formgestaltung (DDR-Begriff für Design) ist vor allem durch ihren ideologischen Auftrag, allgemeine gesellschaftliche Entwicklungen und die sozialistische Planwirtschaft bestimmt worden.

Vom Bauhaus beeinflusste Designer wie der ursprünglich aus den Niederlanden stammende Mart Stam (1948–1950 Rektor der Akademie der Künste und der Hochschule für Werkkunst in Dresden) gaben der sozialistischen Formgestaltung bis Anfang der 50er Jahre eine erste Prägung. Die funktionalistische Gestaltung von Alltagsgegenständen sollte das kulturelle Niveau der Werktätigen heben und ihren Geschmack und ihr Bewusstsein entwickeln. Die Utopie von der Erziehung des neuen Menschen war jedoch weit von einer materiellen Umsetzung entfernt. Die von Kriegszerstörungen und Reparationszahlungen an die Sowjetunion geschwächte ostdeutsche Wirtschaft erzwang die Rationierung von Lebensmitteln und weitgehenden Konsumverzicht. Anfang der 50er Jahre begannen sich die wirtschaftlichen Bedingungen in der DDR leicht zu verbessern. Nach Stalins Tod und dem Arbeiteraufstand 1953 setzte der „neue Kurs" auf Systemlegitimation durch stärkere Konsumorientierung. Walter Ulbricht versprach der Bevölkerung, die BRD bis 1961 in ökonomischer Hinsicht zu überholen. Im Bereich der Formgestaltung wurde auf dem III. Parteitag der SED im Jahr 1950 eine Abkehr vom Funktionalismus vollzogen: Die strenge Ästhetik der Moderne wurde als „Formalismus" gebrandmarkt, der volksfremd und „eine Waffe des Imperialismus" sei. Statt dessen setzte man verstärkt auf Werte der Heimatkunst, das heißt zumeist kitschige Ornamente und Verzie-

Rotkäppchen Sekt
Rotkäppchen sparkling wine
Le vin mousseux *Rotkäppchen*

rungen für die verschiedensten Haushalts-waren. Die stärkere Besinnung auf nationale Elemente – gegenüber der kosmopoliti-schen Orientierung des Funktionalismus – passte auch zur politischen Linie der SED-Führung, die sich in dieser Zeit gern als wahre Protagonistin einer deutschen Wiedervereinigung darstellte.

Dem proklamierten Ziel, die Bundesre-publik in wirtschaftlicher Hinsicht einzuho-len, kam die DDR in den 50er Jahren nicht näher. Statt dessen stieg die Zahl der Über-siedler in die Bundesrepublik immer mehr an. Vom Bau der Berliner Mauer erhoffte sich die SED-Führung eine Konsolidierung der DDR als Staat. Die „guten sechziger Jahre" brachten vielen DDR-Haushalten langlebige Konsumgüter wie Kühlschränke oder Fernsehgeräte. Für die Formgestal-tung eröffnete sich damit ein größeres Betä-tigungsfeld. Die ideologische Verdammung des Funktionalismus wurde wieder relati-viert, das Bauhaus in Dessau renoviert. In der Formgestaltung gab es das Bemühen um eine sozialistische Gegenmoderne mit Anknüpfung an den Funktionalismus. Die Orientierung auf Exportmärkte und das Bemühen, den DDR-Verbrauchern Kon-sumgüter auf „Weltmarktniveau" zu bieten, führte aber auch zunehmend zur Übernah-me von Gestaltungsideen internationaler Produkte. Umgekehrt fanden nicht wenige DDR-Produkte den Weg auf den westdeut-schen Markt, wie zum Beispiel die IKEA-Pendelleuchte aus Halle, die Privileg-Schreibmaschine bei Quelle oder der Fön „Made in GDR".

In den 70er Jahren verstärkte sich die Orientierung auf die möglichst umfassende Erfüllung von Konsumbedürfnissen nach westlichem Vorbild. Dazu zählten auch die Motorisierung der DDR-Gesellschaft mit Trabbi und Wartburg, sowie das Wohnungs-bauprogramm. Der Anspruch auf ein eigen-ständiges sozialistisches Design wurde dabei fast völlig aufgegeben. Die Konsum-kultur des Westens war sowohl für die Bevölkerung der DDR – übertragen durch das „Westfernsehen" – als auch die Partei-führung der Maßstab, der nie erreicht wurde. Die wichtigste Ursache dafür dürfte im Mangel an Konkurrenz und Wettbewerb und den dadurch freigesetzten Triebkräften liegen. Für Unternehmen in marktwirtschaft-lichen Gesellschaften ist ein Überleben nur durch ständige Produkterneuerung und die Produktdifferenzierung zur Konkurrenz möglich. Die Volkseigenen Betriebe der DDR kannten diese Notwendigkeit nicht. Das Styling von Produkten und die Werbung spielten für die DDR-Wirtschaft strukturell eine andere und weniger wichtige Rolle als im Westen. 1960 wurde in der DDR die Wer-besendung „Tausend Tele Tips" gestartet. Sie hatte vor allem die Funktion der Infor-mation und Aufklärung zu Produkten. Älte-ren DDR-Bürgern ist vielleicht der „Fisch-koch" in Erinnerung, der wöchentlich Rezepte zur Verfeinerung der mit kyrilli-schen Zeichen beschrifteten und schwer-verkäuflichen russischen Fischkonserven gab. Diese Form der Produktwerbung wurde 1975 eingestellt. Die sozialistische Planwirtschaft der DDR hatte 40 Jahre lang

p. 10–11: Hutsalon mit Partei-Propaganda
Hat shop with slogan for the 11th Party Congress of the SED: "Fulfil Ernst Thälmann's legacy – help strengthen our socialist fatherland!"

jenen Faktor ausgeschaltet, der in der Bundesrepublik die rasche Innovation der Produkte und des Designs vorangetrieben hatte: den Wettbewerb der Produzenten um die Gunst der Konsumenten.

Nach dem Fall der Mauer im November 1989 verschafften sich viele DDR-Bürger mit dem „Begrüßungsgeld" einen ersten kleinen Vorgeschmack auf die Konsumwelt der Bundesrepublik. Mit der Währungsreform im Sommer 1990 wandten sich die noch-DDR-Bürger in kurzer Zeit fast vollständig von den Konsumprodukten ihrer Volkseigenen Betriebe ab. Niemand wollte mehr Rotkäppchen-Sekt trinken, Club rauchen oder einen Anzug aus „Präsent 20" tragen – „Test the West" lautete das Motto. Innerhalb weniger Wochen nahmen die besseren und bunter verpackten Produkte aus dem Westen die entsprechenden Plätze in den Regalen der ostdeutschen Kaufhallen ein. Mit dem Verschwinden dieser Produkte verschwanden jedoch in der Regel auch die Betriebe und Arbeitsplätze. Ende 1990 hätte kaum jemand vorhersagen können, dass einige der in diesem Buch abgebildeten Produkte noch mal zu einem zweiten Leben erwachen würden. Die schlechte Qualität der DDR-Produkte und ihr verstaubtes Design symbolisierten quasi das gescheiterte DDR-System.

Bereits 1991 setzte jedoch eine erneute Hinwendung der Ostdeutschen zu den tatsächlichen oder vermeintlichen Ost-Produkten ein. Dieser Trend wurde zeitig von westdeutschen Marketingchefs gespürt und genutzt. Club-Cola, seit 1992 wieder in den ostdeutschen Regalen, warb mit „Hurra – ich lebe noch". Die Werbung für die Zigarette „f6" machte deutlich, dass nicht alles aus der DDR vergessen werden sollte: „Der Geschmack bleibt." Die Konkurrenzmarke „Juwel" brachte diese Rückbesinnung auf den Punkt: „Ich rauche Juwel, weil ich den Westen schon getestet hab'". Ost-Produkte konnten in den 90er Jahren in den neuen Bundesländern zum Teil wieder hohe Marktanteile erreichen. So wurde in Thüringen Coca-Cola von Vita-Cola überflügelt. Die „f6" liegt in Ostdeutschland vor allen anderen Marken. In vielen Fällen sind die Produkte erheblich verändert worden und haben mit den originalen DDR-Produkten nur den Namen und einige Design-Anmutungen gemein. Der Trend zu Ostprodukten und die Ostalgie tragen Züge einer Retro-Mode. Sie drücken jedoch auch eine kollektive Ost-Identität und gegenüber der Einheitseuphorie 1990 ernüchterte Erfahrungen mit dem vereinigten Deutschland aus. Davon ist auch das überlegene Design westdeutscher Produkte nicht ausgenommen. „Kathi", der Marktführer für Backmischungen in den neuen Bundesländern, wirbt in einem Werbespot auch mit seiner ost-typischen Verpackung: „Kathi-Packungen haben einen optimalen Auslastungsgrad. Sie sind zu 95 Prozent gefüllt. Der Durchschnitt der Wettbewerber liegt bei nur 55 Prozent. Anders gesagt: 45 Prozent des Packungsinhalts sind bei den Wettbewerbern Luft."

Ralf E. Ulrich

Magasin de chapeaux avec propagande pour le 11ᵉ Congrès du parti SED : « Mettez en valeur l'héritage spirituel d'Ernst Thälmann – fortifiez notre patrie socialiste ! »

9

HUTS

XI.
PARTEITAG

Erfül
E

un

JEDEM
EINE
LEHRSTELLE

INTRODUCTION

In Summer 1989 an exhibition entitled "SED – Schönes Einheitsdesign" (Stunning Eastern Design) opened at the Galerie Habernoll in Dreieich near Frankfurt am Main. The two curators, Matthias Dietz and Christian Habernoll, presented an extensive collection of everyday products from the German Democratic Republic. This not only gave the West German public an insight into the consumer habits of a foreign country. In an indirect way, it also brought visitors face to face with their own post-war experiences. From a West German perspective, many of the East German products on show recalled a time long since past, untouched by costly marketing strategies or sophisticated packaging design. With the fall of the Berlin Wall and currency union in June 1990, East German products like the Trabi, Club-Cola, Juwel cigarettes and Spee washing powder came into direct competition with the VW Golf, Coca-Cola, Camel and Ariel. GDR products had little hope of survival, in their current form and quality. Within a short space of time they mutated into the fossilised remains of a defunct economic and social system.

The products pictured here create a showcase for consumer culture in the former East Germany. The outmoded charm of their shapes, and packaging fascinates modern observers but they are also tangible evidence of a process of stagnation that contributed in no small way to the failure of the GDR. East German design was driven above all by ideology, general social developments and the socialist planned economy.

Until the early 1950s Bauhaus-inspired designers like Dutch-born Mart Stam, who from 1948 to 1950 was rector of the Dresden School of Art and College of Arts and Crafts, made their mark on socialist design. The functional shape of everyday objects was intended to elevate the workers' cultural level and develop their taste and awareness. However, the utopian idea of educating a new kind of citizen was still a long way from being translated into material terms. The East German economy was weakened by the devastation of war and reparation payments to the Soviet Union. This meant that food rationing and large-scale reductions in consumption were inevitable. At the beginning of the 1950s, economic conditions in the GDR began to improve slightly. After Stalin's death and the workers' uprising of 1953, came the announcement of the so-called "New Course", which was more geared to the needs of consumers. Walter Ulbricht promised the population that by 1961 the East German economy would overtake that of the Federal Republic. In the field of design, the 3rd party conference of the SED (Socialist Unity Party) in 1950 rejected the concept of functionalism and branded the austere aesthetics of the modern age as "alien to the people" and "a weapon of imperialism". Instead, greater value was placed on homegrown crafts, which usually meant adorning every type of household item with kitschy motifs. The increased focus on national characteristics – as opposed to the cosmopolitan style of functionalism – was also in line with the political thinking of the SED leadership which, at that time, liked to see itself as playing a crucial role in German reunification.

Schaufenster
Window display: "Apprenticeship for everyone"
Vitrine : « Apprentissage pour tous »

In the 1950s, the GDR came no closer to its declared economic aim of catching up with the Federal Republic. Instead, increasing numbers migrated to West Germany. By building the Berlin Wall, the leaders of the SED hoped to consolidate East Germany's nation status. The halcyon days of the 1960s brought consumer durables like refrigerators and TV sets to many households in the GDR. Design became a much broader area of activity. Less attention was paid to the ideological condemnation of functionalism, and the Bauhaus in Dessau was restored. Designers drew on functionalism in their efforts to develop a socialist alternative to the modern style. However, greater focus on export markets and the desire to offer East Germans consumer goods of "world market standards" led increasingly to the adoption of the design concepts borrowed from international products. On the other hand, quite a few GDR products found their way onto the West German market. They included IKEA pendant lamps made in Halle, Privileg typewriters supplied by the mail order company Quelle and hairdryers "made in the GDR".

The 1970s saw increased attempts to follow the example of the West and do everything possible to meet consumer needs. More and more East Germans took to the roads in their Trabis and Wartburgs, and housing construction programmes went ahead. The quest for an independent socialist form of design was almost completely abandoned. For both ordinary East Germans and the party leadership, western consumer culture — as seen on West German TV channels — was a standard never to be

achieved. This was mostly because there was no rivalry or competition to provide motivation. In order to survive in a market economy, firms must constantly update their products and make them different from those produced by their competitors. The GDR's publicly-owned companies did not recognise this requirement. Compared to their role in the West, product styling and advertising served a quite different and less important function in the East German economy. In 1960 the commercial TV series *Tausend Tele Tips* (A Thousand TV Tips) was launched. Its main purpose was to provide information and advice about different products. Older East Germans perhaps recall the "Fish Cook" who came up with a weekly recipe to make the unpopular Russian fish, sold in cans labelled in Cyrillic script, a little more appetising. This type of product advertising ceased in 1975. For 40 years, the GDR's socialist planned economy had rejected the very factor that in the Federal Republic had forced rapid innovation in products and design: competition between manufacturers to win the favour of consumers.

After the fall of the Wall in 1989 many East Germans used their "welcome money" — an annual gift of DM100 presented from 1987 onwards to GDR citizens visiting the West — to buy themselves a foretaste of the Federal Republic's consumer culture. Following currency reform in Summer 1990, it was not long before East Germans turned completely away from the products made by state-owned companies. Nobody wanted to drink Rotkäppchen sparking wine any more, or smoke Club cigarettes or wear a suit from Präsent 20. The slogan was "Test the West". Within a few weeks, their better and more colourfully packaged West German counterparts took over the shelves of East German shops. However, as products disappeared, so too did firms and jobs. At the end of 1990, few could have predicted that some of the products pictured in this book would be given a new lease of life. The inferior quality and outdated design of East German products seemed to symbolise the failed GDR system.

However, by 1991, Germans in the east of the country were beginning to return to products actually or supposedly produced in the former GDR. West German marketing chiefs quickly caught and exploited the trend. Club Cola, which reappeared on shelves in eastern Germany in 1992, was advertised with the words "Hooray, I'm still alive". The phrase used to publicise f6 cigarettes ("The flavour remains") made it clear that not everything about the old GDR deserved to be forgotten. Juwel, the rival brand, put it in a nutshell with its slogan, "I smoke Juwel because I've already tested the West". By the 1990s, eastern German products had once more captured a considerable market share in the new German states, where f6 outsold all other brands of cigarettes. Many products had undergone dramatic changes and had no more in common with the GDR originals than the name and a few design features. The trend for eastern products and Ostalgie (nostalgia for the former GDR) together bear some of the hallmarks of a retro movement. However, they also express a collective East German identity and a certain disillusionment with united Germany that so contrasts with the euphoria of reunification in 1990. Even the superior design of West German products does not escape criticism. In its commercials, Kathi, the market leader in cake mixes in the new German states, makes claims for its typical East German packaging. Packs of Kathi are filled to optimum capacity. "They are 95 per cent full. On average, competing products are only 55 per cent full. In other words, 45 per cent of the contents of competitors' packaging is no more than air."

Ralf E. Ulrich

PARTEITAG
derSED

INTRODUCTION

Durant l'été 1989, l'exposition « SED – Schönes Einheitsdesign » se déroule à la Galerie Habernoll de Dreieich près de Francfort-sur-le-Main. Les deux commissaires d'exposition Matthias Dietz et Christian Habernoll présentent une vaste collection de produits de tous les jours utilisés en RDA. Pour le public ouest-allemand, c'est l'occasion de découvrir l'univers de la consommation d'un pays étranger, mais les visiteurs sont également confrontés indirectement à leurs souvenirs d'après-guerre, car de nombreux produits exposés évoquent des temps révolus qui n'étaient pas encore marqués par des stratégies de marketing sophistiquées et des emballages au design raffiné. Avec la chute du Mur et l'union monétaire en juin 1990, des articles est-allemands comme le Trabbi, le Club-Cola, les cigarettes Juwel et la poudre à laver Spree entrent en concurrence directe avec la VW Golf, le Coca-Cola, Camel et Ariel. Vu leur forme et leur qualité à l'époque, ces produits ne pourront guère s'imposer et deviendront rapidement les fossiles d'un système économique et social disparu.

Les produits reproduits ici donnent une idée de la culture de la consommation en Allemagne de l'Est. Les formes et les conditionnements au charme désuet fascinent le spectateur d'aujourd'hui out en documentant une stagnation qui a contribué de manière non négligeable à l'échec du système. L'esthétique industrielle socialiste a surtout été déterminée par le message idéologique qu'elle voulait faire passer, les évolutions sociales en général et le dirigisme de l'Etat. Des designers influencés par le Bauhaus, tel Mart Stam d'origine néerlandaise

et qui sera de 1948 à 1950 recteur de l'Académie des beaux-arts et de l'Ecole supérieure des arts appliqués de Dresde, marqueront en un premier lieu le stylisme socialiste jusqu'au début des années 50. L'esthétique fonctionnaliste des objets de tous les jours est censée élever le niveau culturel des travailleurs manuels et développer leur goût et leur conscience. L'éducation de l'homme nouveau reste cependant une utopie fort éloignée des réalités, car l'économie est-allemande, affaiblie par les dévastations dues à la guerre et par le paiement des réparations à l'Union soviétique, fait rationner les produits alimentaires, et contraint à de sévères restrictions sur le plan de la consommation. On note une légère amélioration des conditions économiques au début des années 50.

Après la mort de Staline et l'insurrection des travailleurs en 1953, la « nouvelle ligne politique » mise sur la légitimation du système grâce à une orientation plus forte de la consommation. Walter Ulbricht promet de rattraper l'Allemagne de l'Ouest jusqu'en 1961 sur le plan économique. Dans le domaine de l'esthétique industrielle, la IIIe convention du SED en 1950 se détourne du fonctionnalisme prisé jusque-là, stigmatisant les formes sévères de la modernité qui seraient un « formalisme » étranger au peuple et « une arme de l'impérialisme ». On mise maintenant de manière renforcée sur les valeurs de l'art populaire régional, ce qui signifie le plus souvent des ornements et des décorations kitsch pour les articles ménagers les plus variés. Le retour plus marqué à des éléments nationaux – con-

Schaufenster
Window display
Vitrine

PLASTE
UND
ELASTE
AUS
SCHKOPAU

trairement au fonctionnalisme dont l'orientation était cosmopolite – correspond aussi à la ligne des dirigeants du Parti qui se représentaient volontiers à cette époque comme les vrais protagonistes d'une réunification allemande.

Au cours des années 50, la RDA ne se rapproche pas de l'objectif qu'elle s'est fixé. Au lieu de cela, de plus en plus de citoyens d'Allemagne de l'Est viennent s'établir à l'Ouest. Les dirigeants pensent remédier à cet état de choses en construisant le Mur de Berlin censé consolider la RDA en tant qu'Etat. Les « bonnes années 60 » feront entrer des biens de consommation durables tels des réfrigérateurs ou des postes de télévision dans de nombreux ménages est-allemands. Un champ d'activité plus large s'ouvre ainsi aux stylistes. La malédiction idéologique qui pèse sur le fonctionnalisme est relativisée, le Bauhaus de Dessau restauré. L'esthétique industrielle de l'époque montre que l'on s'applique à créer un mouvement antimoderne attaché au fonctionnalisme. Mais le fait de s'orienter sur des marchés d'exportation et de s'efforcer d'offrir aux consommateurs est-allemands des articles semblables à ceux qui circulent sur le marché mondial, incite de plus en plus à adopter les idées esthétiques qui distinguent ceux-ci. Dans l'autre sens, les produits est-allemands ne seront pas rares à se retrouver sur le marché ouest-allemand ; on peut citer ici, entre autres, le luminaire-pendule IKEA de Halle, la machine à écrire Privileg de Quelle ou le sèche-cheveux « Made in GDR ».

Au cours des années 70, on vise de plus en plus à satisfaire les besoins des consommateurs en se basant sur le modèle occidental. La motorisation de la société est-allemande avec Trabbi et Wartburg fait partie de ce processus ainsi que le programme de construction d'habitations. Ce faisant, l'idée de design socialiste autonome est presque complètement abandonnée. Que ce soit pour la population est-allemande – elle regarde la télévision ouest-allemande – ou la direction du Parti, la culture de consommation telle qu'elle existe à l'Ouest est le standard qui ne sera jamais atteint. La cause majeure en étant l'absence de concurrence et de compétition et des forces motrices qu'elles libèrent. Les entreprises des sociétés d'économie libérale ne peuvent survivre qu'en renouvelant constamment leurs produits et en différenciant ceux-ci des produits concurrents. Les entreprises nationalisées est-allemandes ne connaissent pas cette nécessité. Le stylisme des produits et la publicité jouent ici un autre rôle sur le plan structurel, un rôle moins important qu'à l'Ouest. En 1960, l'émission publicitaire « Tausend Tele Tips » (Mille tuyaux de la télé) est lancée en RDA, qui doit avant tout éclairer le public sur les produits qu'il achète. Les citoyens est-allemands plus âgés se souviennent peut-être du « cuisinier de poisson » qui donnait chaque semaine des recettes pour rendre plus raffinées les préparations en conserve russes étiquetées en signes cyrilliques et difficiles à vendre. Cette forme de publicité

Leuchtreklame an der Transit-Autobahn bei Berlin
Illuminated advertising on the *Transit* motorway leading to Berlin:
"Plastics from Schkopau"
Publicité phosphorescente sur l'autoroute conduisant
à Berlin : « Matières plastiques de Schkopau »

Der *Trabi*, neben dem Wartburg der einzige PKW der DDR;
Wartezeit für einen Neuwagen: bis zu 12 Jahren.
The Trabant, or *Trabi*, besides the Wartburg the only car
available in the GDR; delivery time for a new car: up to
12 years.
La Trabant, ou *Trabi*, avec la Wartburg la seule voiture de
tourisme en RDA ; temps d'attente pour une voiture neuve :
12 ans.

cessera en 1975. Pendant 40 ans, le dirigisme de la RDA aura éliminé le facteur qui a fait avancer en RFA l'innovation rapide des produits et du design : la compétition des producteurs s'affrontant pour gagner les faveurs du consommateur.

Après la chute du Mur en novembre 1989, de nombreux habitants de RDA munis d'un « cadeau de bienvenue » en espèces sonnantes et trébuchantes vont avoir un avant-goût de la consommation telle qu'elle existe à l'Ouest. Avec la réforme monétaire de l'été 1990, ceux qui sont encore des citoyens est-allemands tournent pratiquement le dos aux produits des entreprises nationalisées. Plus personne ne veut boire le crémant Rotkäppchen, fumer des Club ou porter un costume de « Präsent 20 » – la devise est maintenant « Test the West ». En quelques semaines à peine, les articles plus colorés et mieux emballés de l'Ouest supplantent les anciens produits sur les étagères des magasins est-allemands. Mais la disparition de ces articles entraîne celles des entreprises et des emplois – qui aurait pu prédire fin 1990 que certains des produits présentés dans cet ouvrage connaîtrait une renaissance ? La mauvaise qualité des produits est-allemands et leur design obsolète symbolisent pour ainsi dire l'échec du système.

Dès 1991, on note cependant un retour en force des produits véritablement est-allemands ou que les acheteurs tiennent pour tels. Ce trend a été perçu à temps et mis à profit par des responsables marketing ouest-allemands. Club-Cola, de retour dans les étagères de RDA, a annoncé son retour en clamant « Hourra – je vis encore ». La

publicité pour la cigarette « f6 » montre clairement qu'il ne faut pas non plus être trop oublieux : « Le goût reste ». La marque concurrente « Juwel », quant à elle, formule sans ambages : « Je fume Juwel parce que j'ai déjà testé l'Ouest ». Certains produits est-allemands peuvent déjà atteindre de belles parts de marché dans les nouveaux länder. On verra ainsi en Thuringe Coca-Cola battu à plates coutures par Vita-Cola, quant à la « f6 », c'est la première des marques fumées en Allemagne de l'Est. Il faut quand même signaler que dans de nombreux cas, les produits ont été considérablement modifiés et ne partagent plus avec les articles originaux que le nom et certains détails stylistiques.

Le trend des produits est-allemands et l'Ostalgie (la nostalgie de l'Est) ressemblent fort à une mode rétro. Ils expriment cependant aussi une identité collective et, après l'euphorie qui a suivi la réunification, la désillusion qu'éprouvent les Allemands de l'Est. Le design supérieur des produits ouest-allemands fait aussi partie des expériences décevantes : « Kathi », le ténor du marché des préparations à pâtisserie dans les nouveaux länder, apparaît dans un spot publicitaire dans un conditionnement typiquement est-allemand : « Les emballages Kathi ont un degré de capacité optimal. Ils sont remplis à 95 pour cent. La moyenne des concurrents atteint seulement 55 pour cent. Autrement dit : 45 pour cent du paquet sont du vent chez nos concurrents. »

Ralf E. Ulrich

Die Währung der DDR
The GDR currency
La monnaie de la RDA

NAHRUNGSMITTEL
GENUSSMITTEL

FOOD
LUXURY ITEMS

PRODUITS ALIMENTAIRES
DENREES DE LUXE

Cola made in East Germany
Coke made in the GDR
Coca fabriqué en RDA

Alkoholfreies Bier
Non-alcoholic beer
Bière sans alcool

Getränkesirup
Squash
Des Sirops

Erfrischungsgetränke
Soft drinks
Rafraîchissements

p. 30–31
Lebensmittelpräsentation eines HO-Ladens
Display of food in an HO shop
Présentation de denrées alimentaires dans un magasin HO

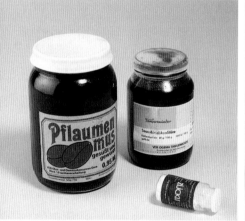

Eingemachtes
Preserves
Conserves

VEB TROCKNUNGSWERK EILSLEBEN

Apfel

Gelee

ELN 177 63210 · HSL 149 542 · ..GL 24055
kJ 1070/190 g   62 Kh/100 g

500 ± 15 g   EVP 1,03 M

Lebkuchen, Speisesalz, Gries, Reis
Gingerbread, salt, semolina, rice
Pain d'épices, sel, semoule, riz

Knäckebrot
Crispbread
Pain suédois

Zwieback
Rusks
Biscottes

Speisestärke
Wheatflour
Fécule de blé

Kartoffelprodukte
Potato products
Préparations à base
de pommes de terre

Eiernudeln
Egg noodles
Pâtes

Getrocknete Hülsenfrüchte
Dehydrated pulse
Légumes secs

Zubereitungshinweise:
Tempo-Bohnen sind nach einem besonderen Verfahren vorbehandelt,
brauchen nicht mehr gewaschen oder eingeweicht
zu werden und sind wie üblich zu verwenden.
Die für die Mahlzeit erforderliche Menge Tempo-
Bohnen in kaltem Wasser oder Brühe ansetzen,
10 Minuten kochen und 5 Minuten ziehen lassen!
Den Vorteil der geringen Kochzeit ausnutzen
und kurzkochende Zutaten, z. B. Fleischkonserven,
oder Würstchen zugeben,
nach Geschmack würzen.

Tempo-
bohnen

nach einem besonderen
Verfahren vorbehandelt
250 g ± 10 g
bei 10 % Restfeuchte

10 MINUTEN KOCHZEIT

250 g

Tempo-
erbsen

nach einem besonderen
Verfahren vorbehandelt
250 g ± 10 g
bei 10 % Restfeuchte

10 MINUTEN KOCHZEIT

250 g

M 0,60

vorschlag:
er
neintopf

fleisch
1 ½ l)

Tempo-
bohnen

Vorgegartes
Rauchfleisch
mitkochen
lassen.
Den Eintopf
mit
Tomatenketchup
sowie
Paprika
pikant würzen.

nach einem besonderen
Verfahren vorbehandelt

250 g ± 10 g
bei 10 % Restfeuchte

10 MINUTEN KOCHZEIT

HSL 13 92 00 0

Eiweiß
24 g

Kohlenhydrate
58 g

Brennwerte
kcal 355
kJ 1486

250 g   M 0,65

SUPPINA

VEB NAHRUNGSMITTELWERKE SUPPINA
9700 AUERBACH

43

Kaffee und Dosenmilch
Roast coffee and tinned milk
Café et lait en boîte

oben/above/en haut:
Puddingpulver, Traubenzucker
Custard powder, corn sugar
Crème en poudre, glucose

unten/below/en bas:
Puddingpulver, Gewürze
Custard powder, spices
Crème en poudre, épices

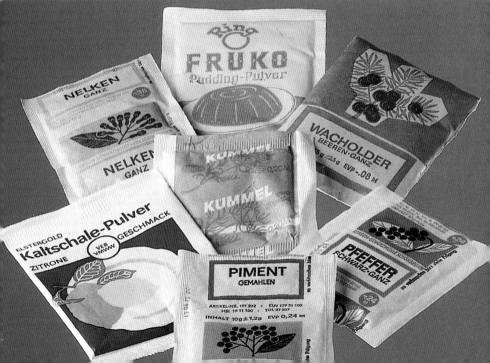

Kindernahrung
Baby food
Alimentation bébé

Kindergries
Baby semolina
Semoule pour bébé

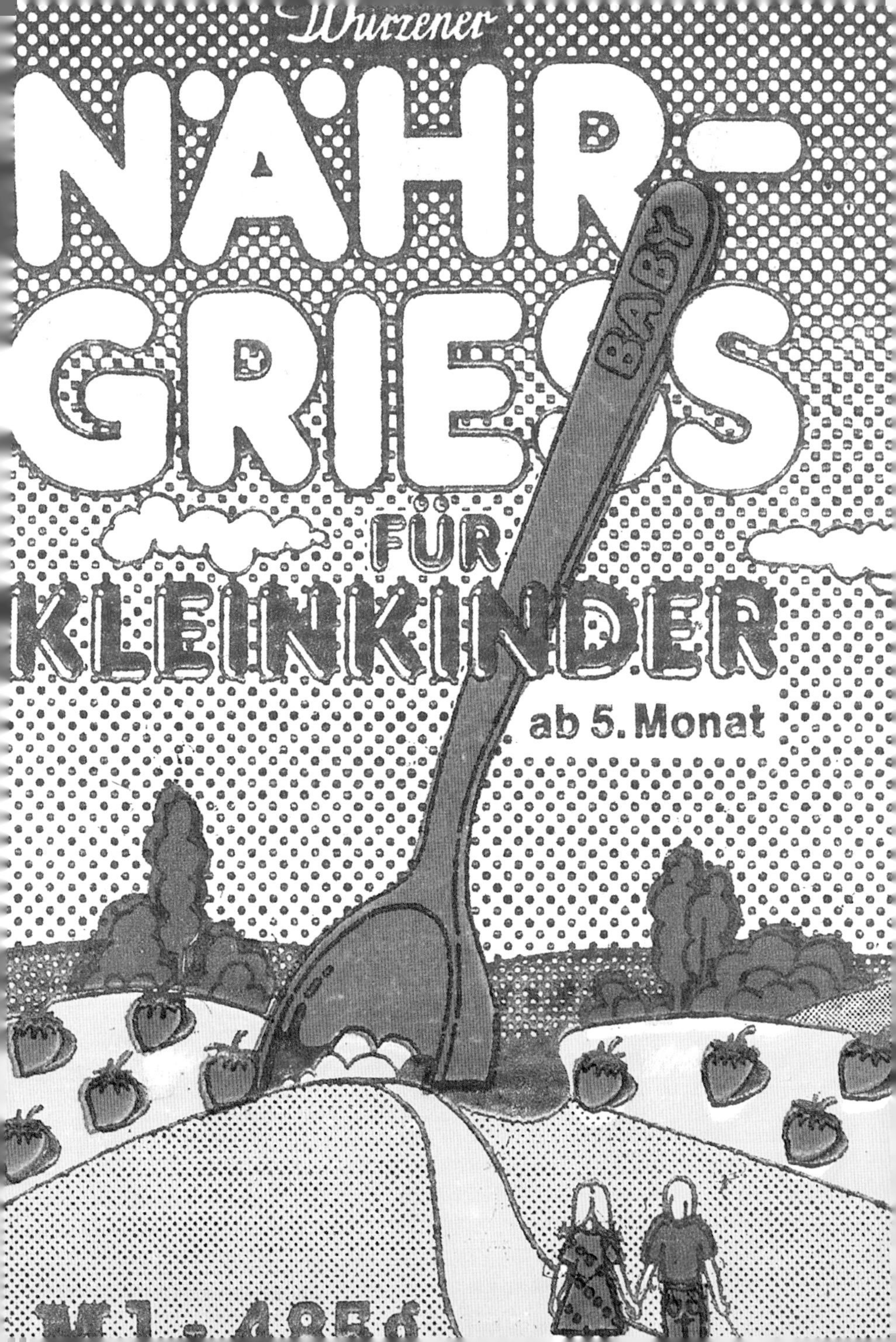
Wurzener
NÄHR-
GRIESS
FÜR
KLEINKINDER
BABY
ab 5. Monat

Drops
Sweets
Bonbons

Waffeln und Kekse
Wafers and biscuits
Gaufrettes et biscuits

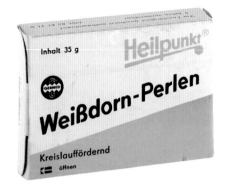

Inhalt 35 g

Heilpunkt®

Weißdorn-Perlen

Kreislauffördernd

öffnen

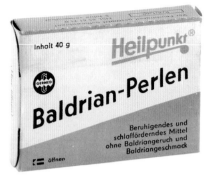

Inhalt 40 g

Heilpunkt®

Baldrian-Perlen

Beruhigendes und
schlafförderndes Mittel
ohne Baldriangeruch und
Baldriangeschmack

öffnen

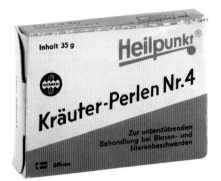

Inhalt 35 g

Heilpunkt®

Kräuter-Perlen Nr.4

Zur unterstützenden
Behandlung bei Blasen- und
Nierenbeschwerden

öffnen

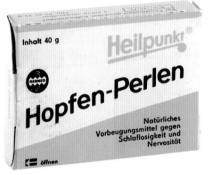

Inhalt 40 g

Heilpunkt®

Hopfen-Perlen

Natürliches
Vorbeugungsmittel gegen
Schlaflosigkeit und
Nervosität

öffnen

Gesundheitskapseln
Health tablets
Dragées sanitaires

Inhalt
35 g

Heilpunkt®

GERMED

Abführ-Perlen

zur Förderung der Verdauung

öffnen

Inhalt 40 g

Heilpunkt®

GERMED

Husten-Perlen

Zur Linderung
von Husten und Heiserkeit

öffnen

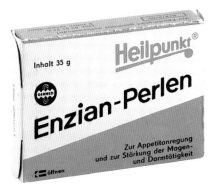

Inhalt 35 g

Heilpunkt®

GERMED

Enzian-Perlen

Zur Appetitanregung
und zur Stärkung der Magen-
und Darmtätigkeit

öffnen

ABFÜHR-PERLEN

ENZIAN-PERLEN

KRÄUTER-PERLEN Nr. 4

HUSTEN-PERLEN

BALDRIAN-PERLEN

WEISSDORN-PERLEN

HOPFEN-PERLEN

jetzt 100 Kapseln

GERMED

Zinsser

Allsat

Knoblauch-Öl-Kapseln

bei Alterserscheinungen und zur Gesundheitspflege

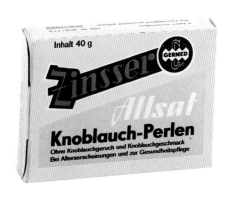

Inhalt 40 g

GERMED

Zinsser

Allsat

Knoblauch-Perlen

Ohne Knoblauchgeruch und Knoblauchgeschmack
Bei Alterserscheinungen und zur Gesundheitspflege

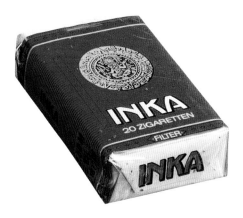

Zigaretten
Cigarettes
Cigarettes

Kautabak
Chewing tobacco
Tabac à chiquer

Zigarren
Speechless cigars
Les cigares *Stupéfiant*

HAUSHALTSWAREN

HOUSEHOLD GOODS

ARTICLES MENAGERS

Besteck aus einem Mitropa Restaurant
Cutlery from a Mitropa Restaurant
Couvert d'un Restaurant Mitropa

Eisbecher-Sets
Sundae sets
Sets de coupes à glace

p. 62
Gummi-Eimer, vulkanisiert
Bucket made of rubber, vulcanized
Seau en caoutchouc, vulcanisé

p. 63
Email-Eimer
Enamel bucket
Seau émaillé

LÖWEN
EMAIL

Thale

TGL 7797

1. WAHL
HSL 65 45 120 EVP 5,05 M

EIERBECHER

6 Stück EVP M 2,10

Eierbecher-Set
Set of eggcups
Set de coquetiers

Eierbecher
Eggcups
Coquetiers

65

Flötenkessel
18 cm, AF, poliert
HSL 65 52 300
ELN 139 15 036
I. Wahl

3,50 M

Pfeffer

Wasserkessel
Whistling kettle
Bouilloire à sifflet

Gewürzstreuer   Eierbecher
Spice shaker   Eggcups
Saupoudreuses   Coquetiers

Eisförmchen
Moulds for making ice-cream
Moules à préparer les glaces en bâtons

68

Eisbecher-Set
Sundae set
Set de coupes à glace

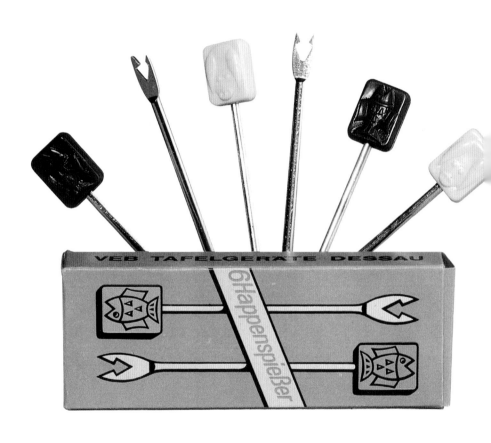

Cocktailspieße
Cocktail sticks
Brochettes cocktail

Partybesteck
Party cutlery
Couverts cocktail

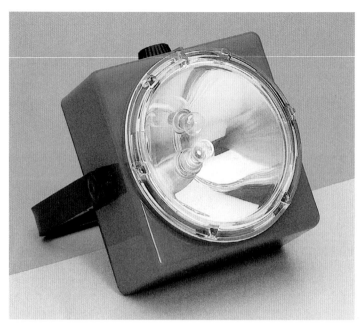

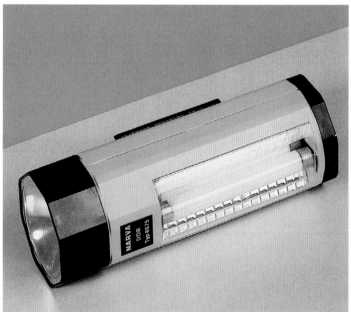

Camping- und Taschenlampen
Torches
Lampes de camping et torches

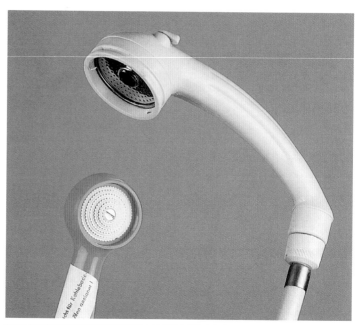

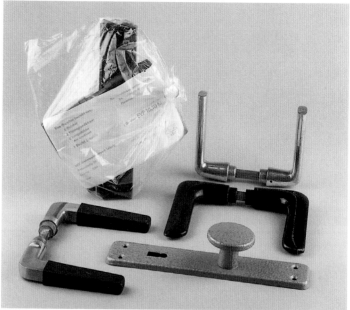

Armaturen, Stecker, Steckdosen, Türgriffe
Fittings, plugs, sockets, door handles
Robinettes, fiches, prises de courant, poignées de porte

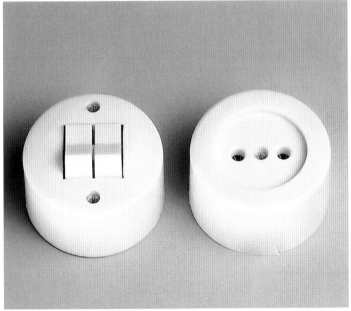

oben/above/en haut:
Gasanzünder
Gas lighter
Briquet à gaz

Taschenmesser
Pocket knife
Couteau de poche

Schwamm
Sponge
Éponge

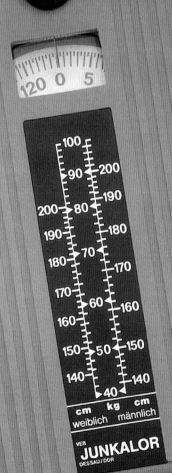

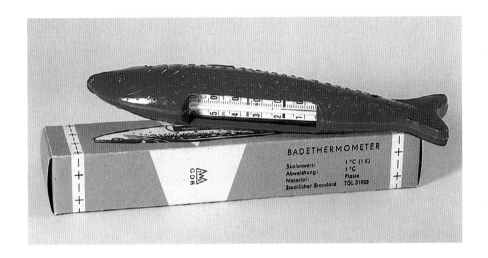

Personenwaage
Bathroom scales
Pèse-personnes

Badethermometer
Bathroom thermometer
Thermomètre

Trinkbecher und Dessertschüsselchen
Cups and dessert bowles
Gobelets et coupelles à dessert

Thermoskanne
Thermos flask
Bouteille thermos

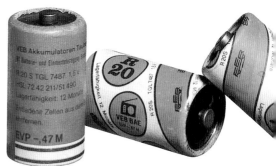

Aschenbecher
Push-down ashtray
Cendrier à évacuation centrifugée

Raucherset
Set for smokers
Set pour le fumeur

Streichhölzer
Matches
Alumettes

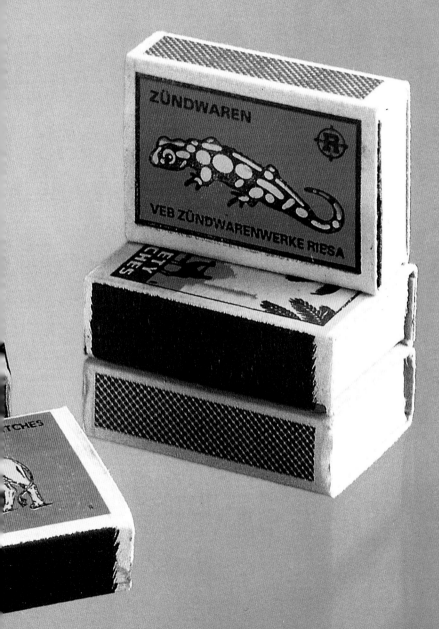

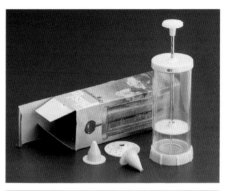

oben/above/en haut:
Einkaufskorb / Garniergerät
Shopping basket / Gadget for icing
Panier / Ustensile à décoration

unten/below/en bas:
Sattelschoner / Dampfkonserviergerät
Covering for bike saddles / Steam preserver
Housse de selle / Appareil à conserver à vapeur

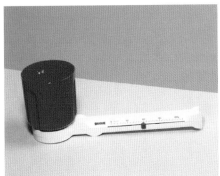

oben/above/en haut:
Stereobrillen / Sonnenblenden
Stereo glasses / Sun shields
Lunettes stéréo / Visières

unten/below/en bas:
Küchenwaage / Butterdose
Kitchen scales / Butter dish
Balance ménagère / Beurrier

oben/above/en haut:
Filter
Filtre

unten/below/en bas:
Serviertabletts
Trays
Plateaux

90

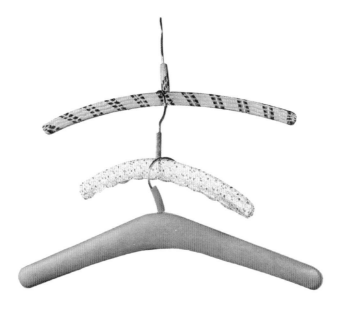

oben/above/en haut:
Handtaschenhalter
Hook for handbags
Crochet pour sacs à mains

unten/below/en bas:
Kleiderbügel
Hangers
Cintres

Verschiedene Verpackungen
Various product packages
Emballages divers

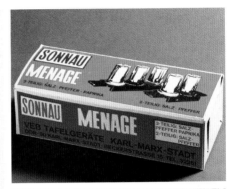

Verschiedene Verpackungen
Various product packages
Emballages divers

ELEKTRISCHE TECHNISCHE OPTISCHE GERÄTE

ELECTRICAL TECHNICAL OPTICAL INSTRUMENTS

APPAREILS ELECTRIQUES TECHNIQUES OPTIQUES

Heizkissen
Heating pad
Coussin chauffant

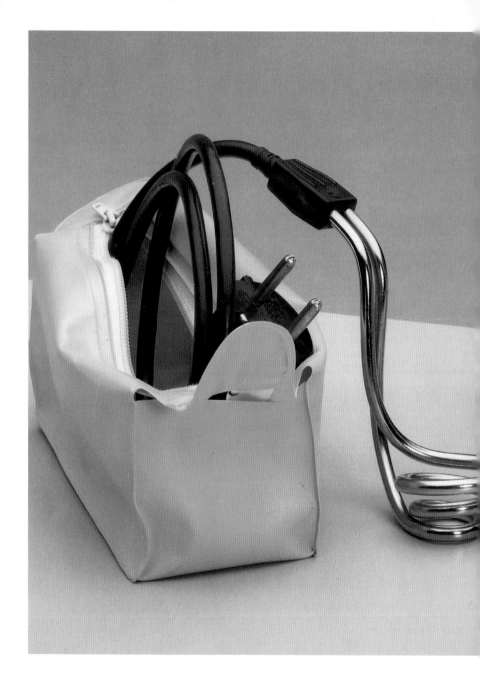

VEB Kontaktbauelemente und Spezialmaschinenbau Gornsdorf

Betrieb im Kombinat
VEB Elektronische Bauelemente

Reisetauchsieder-Garnitur

mit Verpackungstasche, Becher und Bechergriff

220 V / 300 W   ELN 139 22 361   TGL 200-4617
HSL 66 43 6000 1020   **EVP M 16,—**

GARANTIE-SCHEIN

Wir gewähren Ihnen eine den gesetzlichen Bestimmungen
entsprechende Garantie von

6 Monaten

Die Garantieleistung erfolgt ab Verkaufstag an den End-
verbraucher bei auftretenden Mängeln, die nicht durch
einen unsachgemäßen Gebrauch verursacht worden sind.
Bitte beachten Sie hierzu unsere Bedienungsanleitung!
Reparaturen werden nur vom Hersteller ausgeführt.
Rücksendungen bei Garantieansprüchen sind mit ausge-
fülltem Garantieschein an folgende Adresse zu richten:

**VEB Kontaktbauelemente u. Spezialmaschinenbau Gornsdorf
DDR - 9163 Gornsdorf, Auerbacher Straße**

Verkaufstag:

(Stempel und Unterschrift der Verkaufsstelle)

Sorgfältig aufbewahren!   Unausgefüllte Garantiescheine
Bitte wenden!   haben keine Gültigkeit.

Reisetauchsieder mit
Garantieschein
Portable immersion heater
and certificate of guarantee
Chauffe-liquide de voyage
avec bon de garantie

97

Kabeltrommeln aus Bakelit
Cable drums made of bakelite
Tambours de câble en bakélite

Haarföhne
Hair driers
Séche-cheveux

oben/above/en haut:
Wecker
Alarm clock
Réveil

unten/below/en bas:
Reiseschreibmaschine
Portable typewriter
Machine à écrire portable

Telefone
Telephones
Appareils de téléphone

Plattenspieler *Granat*
Record player *Granat*
Tourne disque *Granat*

Fernsehgerät *Debüt*
TV set *Debüt*
Téléviseur *Debüt*

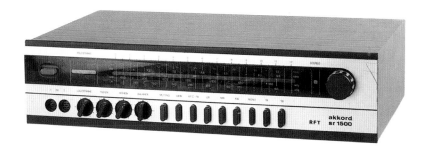

Radio ›akkord‹

Projektor für Diafilme
Projector for slide films
Projecteur de films de diapositives

DEFA-Color-Sonderbildband Nr. 951

Erotica in Weiß und Rot

EVP
11,75 M

DURCHBLICKE

EVP
11,75 M

Toaster

Diaprojektor
Slideprojector
Projecteur de diapositives

Fotoapparate
Cameras
Appareils photos

112

REINIGUNGSMITTEL HYGIENEBEDARF

CLEANSING PRODUCTS COSMETICS

PRODUITS DE NETTOYAGE PRODUITS COSMETIQUES

Scheuermittel (Produkt und Verpackung wurde über 40 Jahre nicht verändert)
Abrasive (product and packaging remained unchanged for over 40 years)
Produit abrasif (produit et emballage n'ont pas été changés pendant 40 ans)

p. 114–115:
Schaufensterauslage eines HO-Ladens mit Reinigungsmitteln
Window display of an HO-shop with cleaning products
Présentation de détergents dans un magasin HO

Haushaltsreiniger
Household cleaner
Produit de nettoyage

Verschiedene Reinigungsmittel
Various cleaning products
Produits de nettoyage divers

Körperpflege
Cosmetics
Produits de soin

118

Rasierwasser	Handcreme	Lotion
After-shave	Hand lotion	
Après rasage	Crème pour mains	

Körperpflege	Intimpflege	Haarwasser
Cosmetics	Personal hygiene	Hair lotion
Produits de soin	Hygiène intime	Lotion capillaire

URA·MOL

Feinmechaniköl F25

HSL 9535500
Inhalt 100 ml

0,45M

TGL 13857
ELN 1324 550

 VEB HYDRIERWERK ZEITZ
Kombinatsbetrieb des
VEB Petrolchemisches Kombinat Schwedt

URA·MOL

Feinmechaniköl F25

HSL 9535500
Inhalt 250 ml

0,80M

TGL 13857
ELN 113 24 550

VEB HYDRIERWERK ZEITZ
Kombinatsbetrieb des
VEB Petrolchemisches Kombinat Schwedt

p. 121–122

Maschinenöl / Feinmechanik-Öl
Lubricating oil / Precision oil
Huile à machines / Huile pour entretien

Schuhputzzeug
Shoe car set
Nécéssaire à chaussures

Schuhcreme: „wenig gesundheitsschädigend"
Shoe polish: "causes little damage to your health"
Cirage : « peu nocif à la santé »

Zahnbürsten
Toothbrushes
Brosses à dents

Zahnpasta
Toothpaste
Dentifice

Seifen
Soap
Savons

Waschmittel
Detergent
Lessive

p. 128–129
Schaufensterdekoration
Window display
Décoration de vitrine

Kinderzahnputzset
Children's dental care set
Nécéssaire dentaire pour enfants

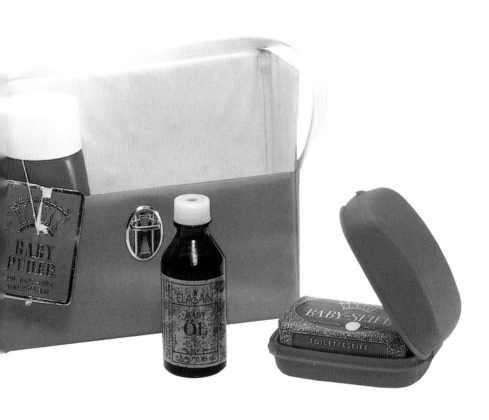

Babypflegeset
Baby care
Nécéssaire de toilette pour bébé

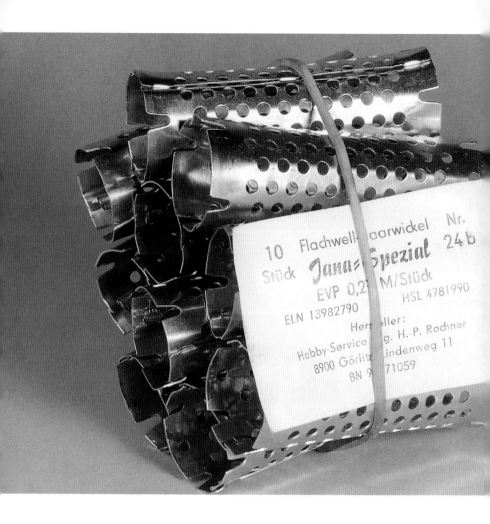

Lockenwickler
Curlers
Bigoudis

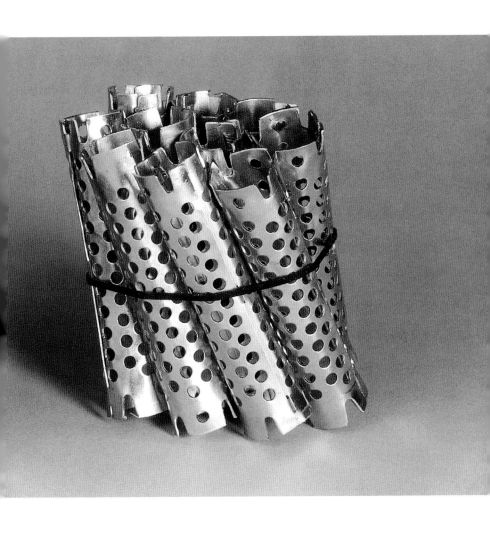

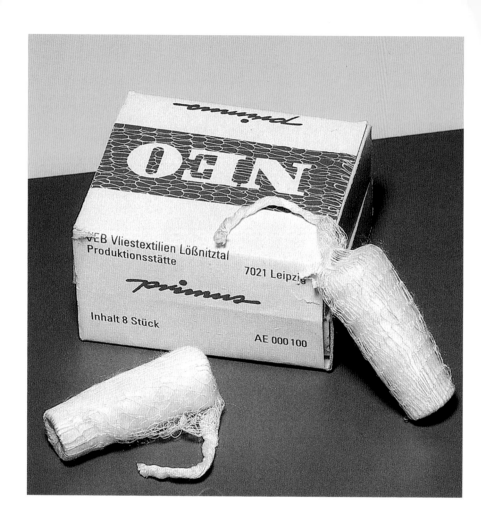

Tampons

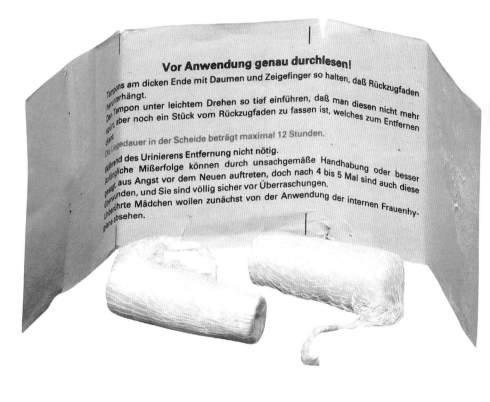

Vor Anwendung genau durchlesen!

Tampons am dicken Ende mit Daumen und Zeigefinger so halten, daß Rückzugfaden herunterhängt.

Den Tampon unter leichtem Drehen so tief einführen, daß man diesen nicht mehr spürt, aber noch ein Stück vom Rückzugfaden zu fassen ist, welches zum Entfernen dient.

Die Liegedauer in der Scheide beträgt maximal 12 Stunden.

Während des Urinierens Entfernung nicht nötig.

Anfängliche Mißerfolge können durch unsachgemäße Handhabung oder besser gesagt, aus Angst vor dem Neuen auftreten, doch nach 4 bis 5 Mal sind auch diese überwunden, und Sie sind völlig sicher vor Überraschungen.

Unberührte Mädchen wollen zunächst von der Anwendung der internen Frauenhygiene absehen.

Tampons und Gebrauchsanleitung
Tampons and instructions for use
Tampons avec mode d'emploi

136

Read carefully before use!
Hold the thicker end of the tampon between your thumb and index finger so that the thread hangs down.
Gently insert the tampon, turning it slightly as you do so, until it can no longer be felt but the thread can be gripped for subsequent removal. Do not leave the tampon inside your vagina for more than 12 hours.
There is no need to remove the tampon when urinating. Initial mishaps may be caused by incorrect insertion or by fear of the new, but at the fourth or fifth attempt difficulties should be a thing of the past and you need expect no more surprises. Virgins should not apply feminine hygiene designed for internal use.

A lire attentivement avant utilisation !
Tenir le tampon hygiénique par l'extrêmité la plus large entre le pouce et l'index en veillant à ce que le fil de retrait pende.
Introduire le tampon dans le vagin en le tournant légèrement, à une profondeur telle que l'on ne le sente plus, mais de manière à ce que l'on puisse encore saisir le fil qui sert à l'enlever. La durée d'utilisation dans le vagin ne doit pas dépasser 12 heures.
Il n'est pas nécessaire d'enlever le tampon pour uriner. Des échecs peuvent se produire au début en raison d'un maniement erroné ou plutôt par peur du nouveau. Toutefois, après 4 ou 5 applications, vous aurez surmonté ces désagréments et ne craindrez plus les mauvaises surprises. Il est souhaitable que les jeunes filles vierges renoncent à l'utilisation de cette protection féminine interne.

Damenfeinstrumpf

maschenlaufhemmend

nahtlos 2,2 tex 20 den

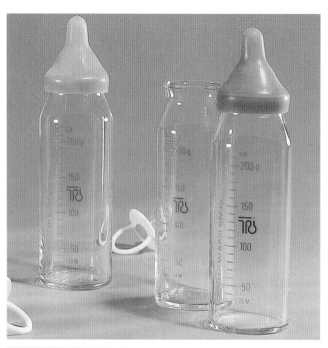

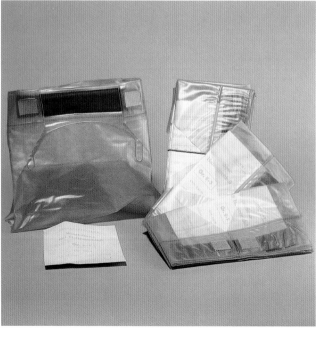

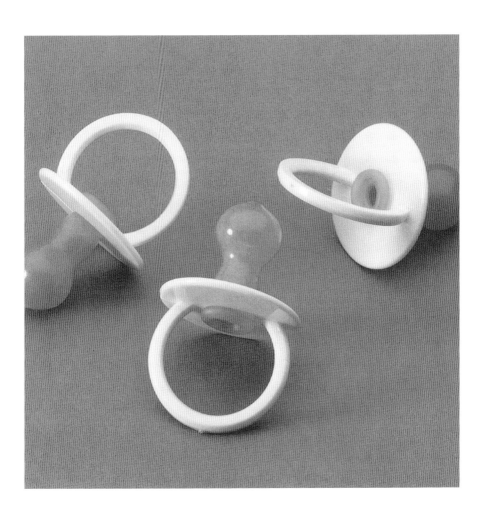

Babyflaschen / Windelhosen aus Plastik
Baby bottles / Plastic nappies
Biberons / Protège-couche en plastique

Schnuller
Dummies
Sucettes

Rasiercreme und Rasierer
Shaving cream and razors
Crème à raser et rasoirs

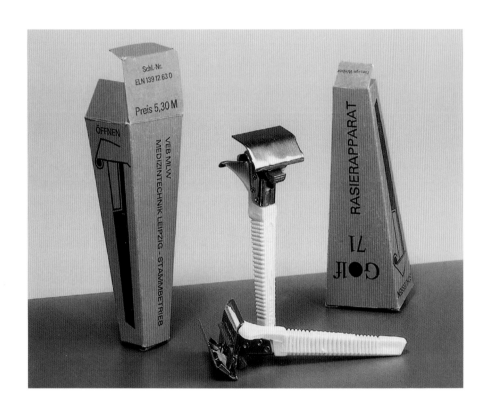

Rasierer
Razors
Rasoirs

Rasierer
Razors
Rasoirs

Inhalt 3 Stück

EVP M 1.—

ELN-Art. Nr.

146 45 160   47706366
Betriebs-Nr. 04 713 010

Bitte verwenden Sie diesen
Abschnitt zum diskreten Einkauf in Ihrem Fachgeschäft.

Heiß vulkanisiert

Lagerfähig bis 1991

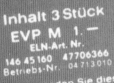

FEUCHT

mondos

aus reinem Naturgummi

Naturgummi

147

typofix ®

Grafischer Spezialbetrieb Saalfeld
Betrieb der VOB Autonis

Siegfried Baumgart
801 Dresden · Altenzeller Str. 50

im Programm

Bestell-Nr. 602

typopress

Verarbeitungshinweis: Schutzpapier entfernen. Auf harter Unterlage mit heiligem Gegenstand (z. B. Kugelschreiber) unter leichtem Druck gleichmäßig anreiben. mit stärkerem Druck nachschreiben bis Buchstabe/Zeichen u. a. grau erscheint. Folie vorsichtig abheben und abgerahmtes Element andrücken.

Lagerungshinweis: Folien hochkantig bei etwa 20° C und einer Luftfeuchte von 60–65% lagern. Lockerung der Folien in Abständen von 2 Wochen notwendig

Blatt 1301   ELN 15 69 2400   7 - 80   V15.3 Mg·G 424· 80   1 Bogen   A 4   5056/T
                                                                EVP   2 35 M

PAPIERE
STOFFE
BÜROBEDARF

PAPER GOODS
MATERIAL
STATIONERY

PAPIERS
TISSUS
PAPETERIE

Rubbelbildchen (Parteiabzeichen)
Rub-on illustrations (party emblems)
Décalcomanie (Insiges du parti)

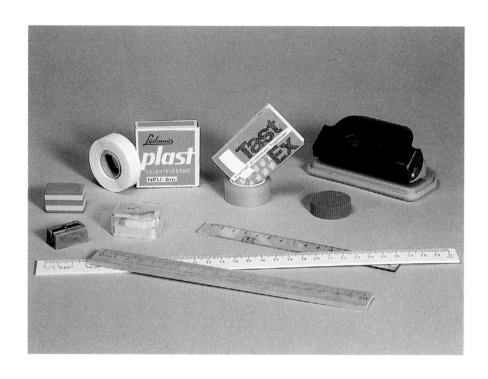

Büroartikel
Stationery
Papeterie

150

Kleber
Glues
Colles

Patronenfüllhalter (Preis für gutes Design)
Fountain pen (Award for Good Design)
Stylo-plume à cartouches (Prix du Bon Design)

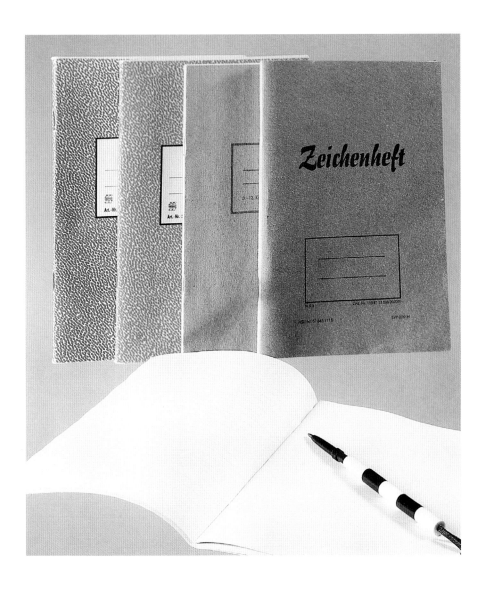

Dem „Vopo"– Knüppel nachempfundener Kuli / Schulhefte
Biro which has the shape of a GDR police club / School notebooks
Stylo bille en forme de matraque de la police de la RDA / Cahiers

Gesetzliche Feiertage 1990

1. Januar	Neujahr
13. April	Karfreitag
15. April	Ostersonntag
1. Mai	Internationaler Kampf- und Feiertag der Werktätigen
3. Juni	Pfingstsonntag
4. Juni	Pfingstmontag
7. Oktober	Nationalfeiertag der DDR
25. Dezember	1. Weihnachtstag
26. Dezember	2. Weihnachtstag

Gedenktage 1990

11. Februar	Tag der Zivilverteidigung
11. Februar	Tag der Werktätigen des Post- und Fernmeldewesens
18. Februar	Tag der Mitarbeiter des Handels
1. März	Tag der Nationalen Volksarmee
8. März	Internationaler Frauentag
21. März	Internationaler Tag für die Beseitigung der Rassendiskriminierung
23. März	Welttag der Meteorologie
27. März	Welttheatertag
7. April	Weltgesundheitstag
8. April	Tag des Metallarbeiters
18. April	Internationaler Denkmalstag
24. April	Internationaler Tag der Jugend und Studenten gegen Kolonialismus und für friedliche Koexistenz
8. Mai	Weltrotkreuztag
10. Mai	Tag des freien Buches
17. Mai	Weltfernmeldetag
18. Mai	Internationaler Museumstag
1. Juni	Tag der Jugendbrigaden
1. Juni	Internationaler Tag des Kindes
5. Juni	Weltumwelttag
10. Juni	Tag des Eisenbahners und Tag der Werktätigen des Verkehrswesens
12. Juni	Tag des Lehrers
16. Juni	Tag der Werktätigen der Wasserwirtschaft
17. Juni	Tag der Genossenschaftsbauern und Arbeiter der sozialistischen Land- und Forstwirtschaft
24. Juni	Tag des Bauarbeiters
1. Juli	Tag der Deutschen Volkspolizei
1. Juli	Tag des Bergmanns und des Energiearbeiters
1. September	Weltfriedenstag
9. September	Internationaler Gedenktag für die Opfer des faschistischen Terrors und Kampftag gegen Faschismus und imperialistischen Krieg
15. September	Tag der Werktätigen des Bereiches der haus- und kommunalwirtschaftlichen Dienstleistungen
1. Oktober	Weltmusiktag
13. Oktober	Tag der Seeverkehrswirtschaft
20. Oktober	Tag der Werktätigen der Leicht-, Lebensmittel- und Nahrungsgüterindustrie
10. November	Weltjugendtag
11. November	Tag des Chemiearbeiters
17. November	Internationaler Studententag
18. November	Tag des Metallurgen
1. Dezember	Tag der Grenztruppen der DDR
11. Dezember	Tag des Gesundheitswesens

VE Kombinat brillant Dresden   EVP 3,90   IK 66/89 05/26/16

Public Holidays 1990

January 1	New Year's Day
April 13	Good Friday
April 15	Easter Sunday
May 1	May Day: International Workers' Day
June 3	Whit Sunday
June 4	Whit Monday
October 7	GDR National Holiday
December 25	Christmas Day
December 26	Boxing Day

Fêtes légales en 1990

1er janvier	Nouvel An
13 avril	Vendredi-Saint
15 avril	Dimanche de Pâques
1er mai	Fête et journée de lutte internationale des travailleurs
3 juin	Dimanche de Pentecôte
4 juin	Lundi de Pentecôte
7 octobre	Fête nationale de la RDA
25 décembre	Noël
26 décembre	Noël

Commemoration Days 1990

February 11	Civil Defence Day
February 11	National Postal and Telecommunications Workers' Day
February 18	National Commerce Day
March 1	National People's Army Day
March 8	International Women's Day
March 21	International Struggle against Racial Discrimination Day
March 23	World Meteorology Day
March 27	World Theatre Day
April 7	World Health Day
April 8	National Metalworkers' Day
April 18	International Monuments' Day
April 24	International Day of Young People and Students against Colonialism and for Peaceful Co-existence
May 8	World Red Cross Day
May 10	National Day of Independant Books
May 17	World Telecommunications Day
May 18	International Museum's Day
June 1	National Youth Brigades' Day
June 1	International Day of the Child
June 5	World Environment Day
June 10	National Railworkers' Day
June 12	National Teachers' Day
June 16	National Waterworkers' Day
June 17	National Collective Farm Workers' and Socialist Agricultural and Forestry Workers' Day
June 24	National Construction Workers' Day
July 1	Day of the German People's Police
July 1	National Mineworkers' and Power Workers' Day
September 1	World Peace Day
September 9	International Memorial Day for the Victims of Fascist Terror and Day of the Struggle against Fascism and Imperialist Wars
September 15	National Domestic and Community Services Workers' Day
October 1	World Music Day
October 13	National Maritime Commerce Day
October 20	National National Light Industry and Food Industry Workers' Day
November 10	World Youth Day
November 11	National Chemical Workers' Day
November 11	International Students' Day
November 18	National Metallurgists' Day
December 1	GDR Frontier Guards' Day
December 11	National Health Service Day

Journées commémoratives en 1990

11 février	Journée de la défense civile
11 février	Journée des travailleurs des postes et télécommunications
18 février	Journée des employés du commerce
1er mars	Journée de l'Armée populaire nationale
8 mars	Journée internationale des femmes
21 mars	Journée internationale pour la suppression de la discrimination raciale
23 mars	Journée mondiale de la météorologie
27 mars	Journée mondiale du théâtre
7 avril	Journée mondiale de la santé
8 avril	Journée des métallurgistes
18 avril	Journée internationale des monuments historiques
24 avril	Journée internationale de la jeunesse et des étudiants contre le colonialisme et pour la coexistance pacifique
8 mai	Journée mondiale de la Croix-Rouge
10 mai	Journée du livre libre
17 mai	Journée mondiale des télécommunications
18 mai	Journée internationale des musées
1er juin	Journée des brigades de la jeunesse
1 er juin	Journée internationale des enfants
5 juin	Journée mondiale de l'environnement
10 juin	Journée des cheminots et des travailleurs du secteur des transports
12 juin	Journée des enseignants
16 juin	Journée des travailleurs du secteur économique des eaux
17 juin	Journée des paysans et travailleurs membres de coopératives socialistes d'agriculture et d'exploitation forestière
24 juin	Journée des travailleurs du bâtiment
1er juillet	Journée de la police populaire allemande
1er juillet	Journée des mineurs et des travailleurs du sector économique de l'énergie
1er septembre	Journée mondiale de la paix
9er septembre	Journée commémorative internationale pour les victimes de la terror fasciste et journée de lutte contre la guerre impérialiste
15 septembre	Journée mondiale des services relatifs aux activités domestiques et communales
1er octobre	Journée mondiale de la musique
13 octobre	Journée des transports maritimes
20 octobre	Journée des travailleurs de l'industrie légère et de l'industrie agro-alimentaire
10 novembre	Journée mondiale de la jeunesse
11 novembre	Journée des travailleurs de l'industrie chimique
17 novembre	Journée internationale des étudiants
18 novembre	Journée des travailleurs de l'industrie métallurgique
1er décembre	Journée des garde-frontière de la RDA
11 décembre	Journée de la santé

Kalenderblatt mit den gesetzlichen Feiertagen der DDR

Calender page with the GDR's public holidays

Feuille de calendrier avec les jours fériés de la RDA

Politwimpel mit den sogenannten Winkelelementen
Code pennants showing the so-called waving elements
Fanions avec les appelés éléments de salut

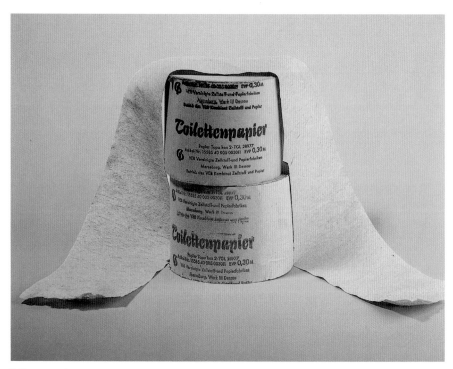

Toilettenpapier
Toilet paper
Papier hygiénique

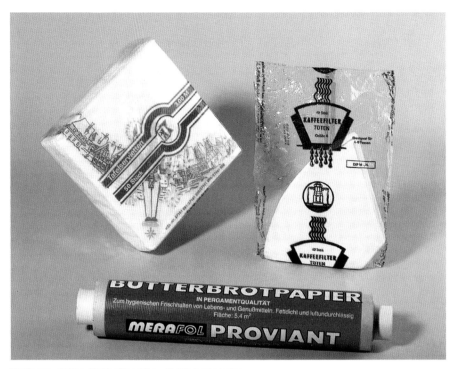

Papierservietten, Kaffeefiltertüten, Butterbrotpapier
Paper napkins, coffee filters, sandwich paper
Serviettes, filtres à café, papier d'emballage de sandwiches

gutgeKauft
im
Fachhandel

Güten
Einkauf

Güten
Einkauf

Einkaufstüten
Shopping bags
Sacs à provisions

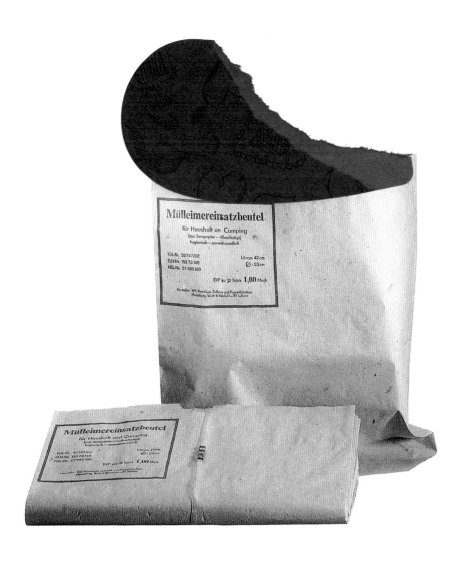

Mülleimerbeutel
Dustbin bags
Sacs poubelles

Einschlagpapier
Wrapping paper
Papier d'emballage

p. 164
Frotteestoff
Terry cloth
Tissu-éponge

p. 165
Kinderzimmertapete
Wallpaper for children's room
Papier peint enfant

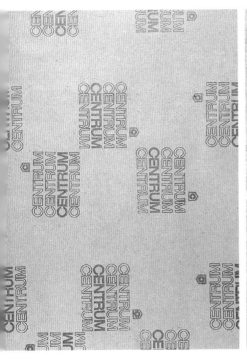

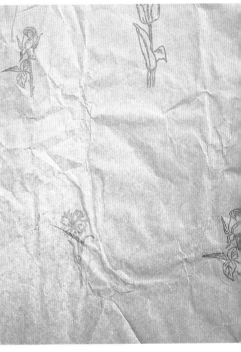

p. 168
Einschlagpapier
Wrapping paper
Papier d'emballage

p. 169
Krawatten
Ties
Cravates

p. 170
Tapeten
Wallpapers
Papiers peints

p. 171
Stoffe
Textiles
Tissus

SPIELWAREN

TOYS

JOUETS

Spielesammlung
Set of games
Coffret de jeux

Mensch ärgere dich nicht
Ludo
Jeu de petits chevaux

Wundertüten
Surprise bags
Pochettes surprise

Bastelbogen
Cut-and-paste kit
Maquettes de bricolage

Ausschneidebögen
Cut-outs
Maquettes à découper

JOSEPHINE

177

VEB Kleinpuppen Lic
Schlüssel-Nr. 182 33
Artikel-Nr. 543100
EVP 6,00 M

Puppen
Dolls
Poupées

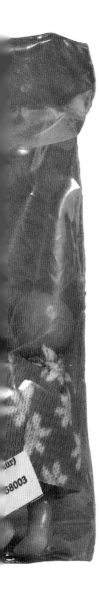

Spielzeugwaage
Toy scales
Balance miniature

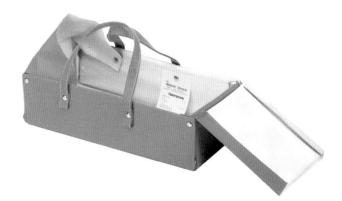

Puppentrage
Doll's carriage
Couffin de poupée

Herr Fuchs
Mister Fox
Monsieur Renard

Schnatterinchen

Frau Elster
Mrs Magpie
Madame Pie

Sandmännchen
Sandman
Marchand de sable

Pittiplatsch

Figuren aus dem Kinderfernsehen
Figures from children's TV
Personnages de la télévision pour enfants

Fußballmaskottchen
Football mascot
Mascotte de football

Spardosen
Money boxes
Tirelires

Seeleute
Seamen
Marins

Würfelspiel
Boardgame
Jeu de dés

Polizeiauto im amerikanischen Stil   Spielzeugampel   Spielzeugautos
Police car in American style   Model traffic light   Model cars
Voiture de police en style américain   Feu tricolore miniature   Voitures miniatures

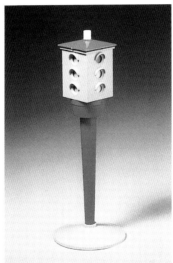

HISTORISCHER ÜBERBLICK ÜBER DAS DDR DESIGN

1945 Gründung der Arbeitsgemeinschaft *Formgebung* in Weimar unter Leitung von Horst Michel.

1946 Offizielle Wiedereröffnung der Hochschule für Baukunst und Bildende Künste in Weimar. Der Architekt Hermann Henselmann wird zum Direktor berufen und mit der Reorganisation der Hochschule beauftragt.

1948 Mart Stam wird damit beauftragt, die bisherige Hochschule für Werkkunst in Dresden auszubauen und diese mit der Akademie der Künste zu vereinen.

1950 In Berlin wird unter Mart Stam das *Institut für Industrielle Gestaltung (IFIG)* gegründet, das der Kunsthochschule Berlin-Weißensee angeschlossen ist.

1951 Gründung des Instituts für Innengestaltung an der nun in *Hochschule für Architektur und Bauwesen* umbenannten Weimarer Ausbildungsstätte.

1952 Umbenennung des *IFIG* in *Institut für Angewandte Kunst (Ifak)*.

1954 Erste staatliche Anordnung, der *Beschluss des Ministerrates über die neuen Aufgaben der Innenarchitektur und der Möbelindustrie,* weist dem Weimarer Institut besondere Verantwortungsbereiche zu.

1955 Weimarer Institut beteiligt sich mit einer Sonderschau an der Münchener Ausstellung *Ernährung und Wohnkultur.*

1956 Herausgabe des 1. Heftes der DDR-Fachzeitschrift für industrielle Gestaltung *form & zweck* (zunächst als Jahrbuch, ab 1964 als Zeitschrift).

1957 Weimarer Institut stellt bei der XI. Mailänder Triennale aus und stößt damit auf ein großes Echo in westeuropäischen Medien.

1972 Gründung des staatlichen *Amtes für Industrielle Formgestaltung (AIF)* mit der Funktion, aktuelle Designprozesse in der Industrie zu lenken und zu verwalten. Leiter ist Dr. Martin Kelm.

1976 Gründung des *Wissenschaftlich-Kulturellen Zentrums Bauhaus Dessau.*

1978 Schaffung der staatlichen Auszeichnung *Gutes Design* (wird zur Internationalen Leipziger Messe zweimal jährlich vergeben).

1988 Das AIF präsentiert in Stuttgarts Design Center mit der Ausstellung *Design in der DDR* erstmals einen Überblick zur ostdeutschen Designgeschichte.

1989 Eröffnung der Ausstellung *SED – Schönes Einheits Design* in der Galerie Habernoll in Dreieich bei Frankfurt/Main. Seit 1999 befindet sich diese Sammlung der verschiedensten DDR-Konsumgüter als Dauerleihgabe im Haus für Geschichte, Leipzig.

1990 Auf der Leipziger Frühjahrsmesse wird zum letzten Mal die Auszeichnung *Gutes Design* vergeben.

1993 Unter dem Titel *Neue Länder Neue Wege* veranstaltet das Internationale Design Zentrum Berlin eine umfassende Wanderausstellung mit Design-Innovationen aus den ostdeutschen Bundesländern.

1999 Präsentation von *DDR-Alltagskultur* auf der Berliner Ausstellung *Wege der Deutschen* im Martin-Gropius-Bau.

HISTORICAL OVERVIEW OF EAST GERMAN DESIGN

1945 Design study group led by Horst Michel set up in Weimar.

1946 Official reopening of the College of Architecture and Fine Arts in Weimar. The architect Hermann Henselmann is appointed director, with the task of reorganising the institution.

1948 Mart Stam is given the task of expanding the existing college of arts and crafts in Dresden and amalgamating it with the city's academy of arts.

1950 The Industrial Design Institute, connected to the Berlin-Weißensee college of art and headed by Mart Stam, is founded in Berlin.

1951 Foundation of the Interior Design Institute within the college of architecture in Weimar, now renamed the College of Architecture and Construction

1952 The Industrial Design Institute is renamed the Institute for Applied Arts.

1954 The first official directive, the "Resolution of the Council of Ministers on the New Functions of Interior Design and the Furniture Industry", gives special responsibilities to the institute in Weimar.

1955 The Weimar institute stages a special exhibition at the *Nutrition and Home Décor* exhibition in Munich.

1956 Publication of the first issue of the East German technical journal for industrial design *form & zweck* (initially published as a yearbook, then from 1964 onwards as a journal).

1957 The Weimar institute takes part in the 11th Milan Triennale, attracting a big response from the West European media.

1972 The government sets up a Depart-
ment of Industrial Design whose function is to oversee and administer current design processes in industry. The department is headed by Dr. Martin Kelm.

1976 Bauhaus Dessau Scientific and Cultural Centre founded.

1978 The government creates the official *Good Design* Award (presented twice yearly at the Leipzig International Trade Fair).

1988 At the *Design in the GDR* exhibition at the Design Centre in Stuttgart, the Department of Industrial Design presents a first-ever survey of the history of design in East Germany.

1989 The exhibition *SED – Stunning Eastern Design* opens at the Galerie Habernoll, Dreieich near Frankfurt am Main. Since 1999 this highly varied collection of East German consumer goods has been on long-term loan to the Haus der Geschichte, Leipzig.

1990 The *Good Design* Award is presented for the last time at the Spring Trade Fair in Leipzig.

1993 Under the title *New States New Ways* the International Design Centre in Berlin organises an extensive mobile exhibition of design innovations from the East German federal states.

1999 *Everyday Life in the GDR* is presented as part of the *German Pathways* exhibition at the Martin-Gropius-Bau, Berlin.

HISTOIRE DU DESIGN EN RDA

1945 Fondation du cercle d'études *Form-gebung* à Weimar sous la direction de Horst Michel

1946 Réouverture officielle de l'Ecole supérieure d'architecture et d'arts plastiques de Weimar. L'architecte Hermann Henselmann est nommé directeur et est chargé de réorganiser l'école.

1948 Mart Stam est chargé de développer l'Ecole supérieure des arts appliqués de Dresde et de l'unir à l'Académie des beaux-arts.

1950 L'Institut de design industriel (*Institut für Industrielle Gestaltung, IFIG*) est fondé à Berlin sous la direction de Mart Stam. Il est rattaché à l'Ecole supérieure des beaux-arts de Berlin-Weißensee.

1951 Création de l'institut de design intérieur (*Institut für Innengestaltung*) dans ce qui est maintenant nommé l'Ecole supérieure d'architecture et de construction de Weimar (*Hochschule für Architektur und Bauwese*).

1952 L'institut de design industriel *IFIG* est rebaptisé institut des arts appliqués (*Institut für Angewandte Kunst, Ifak*).

1954 Premier décret d'Etat, la résolution du conseil ministériel sur les nouvelles tâches de l'architecture intérieure et de l'industrie du meuble attribue à l'institut de Weimar des domaines de responsabilité particuliers.

1955 L'institut de Weimar participe à l'exposition munichoise *Ernährung und Wohnkultur* (Alimentation et culture de l'habitat)

1956 Parution du premier cahier de *form & zweck*, une publication est-allemande spécialisée dans l'esthétique industrielle (d'abord en tant qu'annuaire, puis sous forme de revue à partir de 1964).

1957 L'institut de Weimar expose à la XIe Triennale de Milan, ce qui provoque un vaste écho dans les médias d'Europe de l'Ouest.

1972 Fondation du bureau national du design industriel (*Amtes für Industrielle Formgestaltung, AIF*). Il est chargé de guider et d'administrer les processus actuels de design dans l'industrie. Il est dirigé par le Dr Martin Kelm.

1976 Fondation du Centre scientifico-culturel du Bauhaus de Dessau (*Wissenschaftlich-Kulturellen Zentrums Bauhaus Dessau*).

1978 Création de la distinction nationale *Gutes Design* (octroyée deux fois par an à la foire internationale de Leipzig).

1988 Avec l'exposition *Design in der DDR*, la AIF présente pour la première fois au Design Center de Stuttgart une vue d'ensemble de l'histoire du design est-allemand.

1989 Inauguration de l'exposition *SED – Schönes Einheits Design* à la Galerie Habernoll de Dreieich près de Francfort-sur-le-Main. Depuis 1999 cette collection des produits de consommation est-allemands les plus divers est abritée en tant que prêt durable par la Haus für Geschichte de Leipzig.

1990 La décoration *Gutes Design* est attribuée pour la dernière fois à la foire de printemps de Leipzig.

1993 Le Centre de Design international de Berlin organise une exposition ambulante intitulée *Neue Länder Neue Wege*, qui présente des innovations esthétiques originaires des régions est-allemandes de la République fédérale.

1999 Présentation de *DDR-Alltagskultur* à l'exposition berlinoise *Wege der Deutschen* dans le Martin-Gropius-Bau.

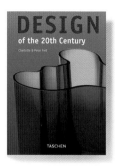

Design of the 20th Century
Charlotte & Peter Fiell / Flexi-
cover, Klotz, 768 pp. / € 19.99 /
$ 29.99 / £ 16.99 / ¥ 3.900

Industrial Design A-Z
Charlotte & Peter Fiell / Flexi-
cover, Klotz, 768 pp. / € 19.99 /
$ 29.99 / £ 14.99 / ¥ 3.900

Designing the 21st Century
Ed. Charlotte & Peter Fiell /
Flexi-cover, 576 pp. / € 29.99 /
$ 39.99 / £ 19.99 / ¥ 4.900

"... a thorough overview of design highlights of the last 100 years, with lavish illustrations and user-friendly cross references."

—*Building Design,* London, on *Design of the 20th Century*

"Buy them all and add some pleasure to your life."

All-American Ads 40ˢ
Ed. Jim Heimann

All-American Ads 50ˢ
Ed. Jim Heimann

All-American Ads 60ˢ
Ed. Jim Heimann

Angels
Gilles Néret

Architecture Now!
Ed. Philip Jodidio

Art Now
Eds. Burkhard Riemschneider,
Uta Grosenick

Atget's Paris
Ed. Hans Christian Adam

Berlin Style
Ed. Angelika Taschen

Best of Bizarre
Ed. Eric Kroll

Bizarro Postcards
Ed. Jim Heimann

Karl Blossfeldt
Ed. Hans Christian Adam

California, Here I Come
Ed. Jim Heimann

50ˢ Cars
Ed. Jim Heimann

Chairs
Charlotte & Peter Fiell

Classic Rock Covers
Michael Ochs

Description of Egypt
Ed. Gilles Néret

Design of the 20ᵗʰ Century
Charlotte & Peter Fiell

Design for the 21ˢᵗ Century
Charlotte & Peter Fiell

Dessous
Lingerie as Erotic Weapon
Gilles Néret

Devils
Gilles Néret

Digital Beauties
Ed. Julius Wiedemann

Robert Doisneau
Ed. Jean-Claude Gautrand

East German Design
Ralf Ulrich / Photos: Ernst Hedler

Eccentric Style
Ed. Angelika Taschen

Encyclopaedia Anatomica
Museo La Specola, Florence

Erotica 17ᵗʰ–18ᵗʰ Century
From Rembrandt to Fragonard
Gilles Néret

Erotica 19ᵗʰ Century
From Courbet to Gauguin
Gilles Néret

Erotica 20ᵗʰ Century, Vol. I
From Rodin to Picasso
Gilles Néret

Erotica 20ᵗʰ Century, Vol. II
From Dali to Crumb
Gilles Néret

Future Perfect
Ed. Jim Heimann

The Garden at Eichstätt
Basilius Besler

HR Giger
HR Giger

Homo Art
Gilles Néret

Hot Rods
Ed. Coco Shinomiya

Hula
Ed. Jim Heimann

India Bazaar
Samantha Harrison,
Bari Kumar

Indian Style
Ed. Angelika Taschen

Industrial Design
Charlotte & Peter Fiell

Japanese Beauties
Ed. Alex Gross

Kitchen Kitsch
Ed. Jim Heimann

Krazy Kids' Food
Eds. Steve Roden,
Dan Goodsell

Las Vegas
Ed. Jim Heimann

London Style
Ed. Angelika Taschen

Male Nudes
David Leddick

Man Ray
Ed. Manfred Heiting

Mexicana
Ed. Jim Heimann

Native Americans
Edward S. Curtis
Ed. Hans Christian Adam

New York Style
Ed. Angelika Taschen

**Extra/Ordinary Objects,
Vol. I**
Ed. Colors Magazine

**Extra/Ordinary Objects,
Vol. II**
Ed. Colors Magazine

15ᵗʰ Century Paintings
Rose-Marie & Rainer Hagen

16ᵗʰ Century Paintings
Rose-Marie & Rainer Hagen

Paris-Hollywood
Serge Jacques
Ed. Gilles Néret

Paris Style
Ed. Angelika Taschen

Penguin
Frans Lanting

Photo Icons, Vol. I
Hans-Michael Koetzle

Photo Icons, Vol. II
Hans-Michael Koetzle

20ᵗʰ Century Photography
Museum Ludwig Cologne

Pin-Ups
Ed. Burkhard Riemschneider

Giovanni Battista Piranesi
Luigi Ficacci

Provence Style
Ed. Angelika Taschen

Pussycats
Gilles Néret

Redouté's Roses
Pierre-Joseph Redouté

Robots and Spaceships
Ed. Teruhisa Kitahara

Seaside Style
Ed. Angelika Taschen

Albertus Seba. Butterflies
Irmgard Müsch

**Albertus Seba. Shells &
Corals**
Irmgard Müsch

See the World
Ed. Jim Heimann

Eric Stanton
Reunion in Ropes & Other
Stories
Ed. Burkhard Riemschneider

Eric Stanton
She Dominates All & Other
Stories
Ed. Burkhard Riemschneider

Sydney Style
Ed. Angelika Taschen

Tattoos
Ed. Henk Schiffmacher

Tuscany Style
Ed. Angelika Taschen

Edward Weston
Ed. Manfred Heiting

Women Artists
in the 20ᵗʰ and 21ˢᵗ Century
Ed. Uta Grosenick